The Quest of Captain Cook

Stone Hatchet,
Tahiti

The Quest of
Captain Cook

BY MILLICENT E. SELSAM

ILLUSTRATED BY LEE J. AMES

DOUBLEDAY & COMPANY, INC.   •   GARDEN CITY, NEW YORK

Other Books in This Series

Library of Congress Catalog Card Number 62-7072

Carved Tortoise-Shell Ornament
upon Conch Shell,
Pacific Islands

Contents

James Cook

The Quest

Today, great lumbering machines carry teams of men across the frozen Antarctic Continent while airplanes fly over its icy mountains. Nuclear-powered submarines dive under the arctic ice off the coast of Alaska, cross the North Pole and surface in the Greenland Sea on the other side of the earth. Australia and New Zealand are important modern nations. Hawaii and Alaska are states of the United States.

Two hundred years ago the Antarctic Continent was unknown. Alaska was scarcely more than a glint in the eye of Russian fur traders. Hawaii was on no map. No one knew whether or not ships could pass from ocean to ocean through the Arctic Sea. Australia and New Zealand were undefined globs of land. Thousands of miles of the vast Pacific and its islands were

7

unknown to Europeans. And, as is always the case, when men do not know what things really are their imagination plays tricks on them. Many learned men firmly believed that there was a great unknown continent in the Southern Hemisphere to balance that of Europe and Asia in the Northern one.

In the years from 1768 to 1779 James Cook sailed in three great voyages around the world. The story of these voyages is the story of the greatest single quest any man ever made to explore uncharted waters and to discover real lands in place of imaginary ones. He mapped all the coast of New Zealand and eastern Australia and claimed these lands for the British crown. He discovered innumerable islands in the Pacific and rediscovered others that mariners had once reached but couldn't find again. He circumnavigated the Antarctic and found ample reasons to believe there was a continent there. He discovered the Hawaiian Islands. He mapped the northwest coast of America and sailed into the Arctic Ocean in search of a passage east or west.

But all Cook's discoveries, as great as they were, are only a part of the story. He was not a conqueror, marauder, bandit or pirate, as so many navigators before him had been. Cook was a navy man devoted to the arts of peace. The achievement of which he was proudest was the conquest of scurvy, the dread disease of the sea that had ruined so many previous voyages. During ten years of perilous journeyings Cook kept his men healthy as sailors had never been before. He instituted his own "public health service" that made life on his ships, in cramped quarters and in all weather, a better "risk" than in the England of his day.

Cook's quest also converted navigation from an art into a science. His three voyages mark the dividing line between the dauntless ocean adventurers of the preceding centuries and the systematic exploration of the earth that has taken place since. Columbus, Vasco da Gama, Magellan, and Tasman, among others, had been most able and courageous sailors, but often enough did not know just where they were on the earth and how to get there again. Cook had new instruments and used them so skillfully that he could determine his exact position on the earth almost any hour of the day or night. He opened a new era of scientific navigation and oceanography.

James Cook's three great voyages reveal not only a scientifically minded sailor but also a humane civilized man who believed that all peoples could learn from one another and live in peace. He sought to advance the interests of his country and to serve mankind as a whole. But above all he was an explorer, driven on by an intense desire to go "not only farther than any other man has been before me, but as far as I think it possible for man to go."

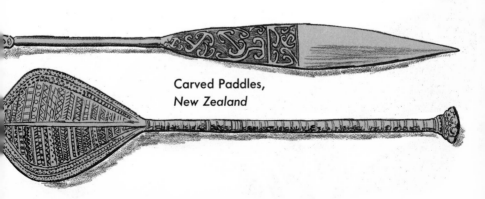

Carved Paddles,
New Zealand

A Commander Wanted

James Cook's famous voyages originated in a decision of the *Royal Society of London for the Improvement of Natural Knowledge*. On a November afternoon in 1767 there was an excited hush in the council room of the Society. The chairman of a special committee had taken the floor to give his report. There was great interest in what he would have to say. The year 1769 promised to be an unusually exciting one for astronomers. An event would take place in the heavens that would not occur again for a century. The great astronomer Edmund Halley had predicted that the planet Venus would pass across the face of the sun in 1769. Halley's predictions had to be taken seriously. He had observed the great comet of 1682 and predicted that it

11

would appear again at Christmas time, 1758. It did, and has been called Halley's comet ever since.

The transit of Venus interested the Royal Society, as it did scientific bodies in many countries. Halley had shown that careful observations of it would provide a means of determining accurately the earth's distance from the sun. This figure would then enable astronomers to calculate the dimensions of the whole solar system. The Council of the Society had set up a committee to study where and how these observations could best be made.

The chairman reported that to get useful measurements of the transit of Venus, observations would have to be made from three points on the earth: one at the northern tip of Norway, another in the region of Hudson Bay, the third in the middle of the South Sea, as the Pacific Ocean was then called.

The first two of these would be easy. But the third? How could they get a ship to the middle of the South Sea? And who would represent the Society as its observer?

The Committee had its answers ready. They would

appeal to King George for help in getting a ship. As their observer they recommended Mr. Alexander Dalrymple "as an able navigator and well skilled in astronomical observation."

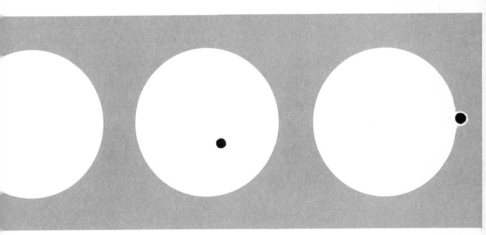

The transit of Venus

The recommendations were immediately approved. King George was interested in the Society's work and could be counted on to support it. And Dalrymple, one of the Royal Society's distinguished members, seemed a happy choice. He was not only a good astronomer but had also commanded a merchantman in the Far East. He was a scholar, too, who had devoted years to the study of all available records of South Sea explorations. Besides, he was the leader of the popular idea that there was a great southern continent in the Pacific Ocean. This continent had not yet been discovered but Dalrymple was sure it was there waiting to be found.

Shortly afterward the Council received Mr. Dalrymple's reply. "I accept," it said, "but I must make it clear that I can have no thought of undertaking the voyage as a passenger, or on any other footing than being in command of the ship intended for the service."

King George III agreed to provide the Society with a ship and promised a large sum of money to finance the scientific expedition. The office of the British Admiralty received a special communication from the King on February 29, 1768. It was asked to provide a naval ship for the voyage to the Pacific. This it could easily do. But who would command it?

Lord Merton, president of the Royal Society, called on Sir Edward Hawke, First Lord of the Admiralty, to request the appointment of Mr. Alexander Dalrymple to command the South Sea vessel. The response was a decisive "No!"

The Admiralty had some ideas of its own about this voyage. The Spanish, French, Portuguese, and Dutch had been more active in Pacific exploration during the century than the British had. Commodore Byron had just crossed the Pacific, but his ship was the first the British had there in twenty-five years. Another voyage, under Captain Wallis, was on its way home from that area now, but efforts had to be intensified. If there were a southern continent, the country that discovered it would be the mistress of the seas. If there were not, the sooner Britain knew it the better. Besides, there was trouble brewing in the American colonies, and new overseas possessions could prove crucial for Britain's whole future. The Admiralty wanted a naval man, not a civilian, as commander. They wanted a man who could map unknown coasts on a long voyage with secret instructions and no time limit. But under the agreement the King had made with the Royal Society, this man would have to be approved by them.

The negotiations over a commander were at a standstill.

Then Mr. Philip Stevens, secretary of the Admiralty, suggested James Cook for the command.

The Lords of the Admiralty barely knew who Cook was. He had never been to the Pacific. He had never been anywhere outside of North American waters. He didn't even have a commission. And would the Royal Society accept him?

The Admiralty looked into its records. They revealed that James Cook had enlisted in the navy as an able-bodied seaman in 1755 at the age of twenty-seven. He had spent ten years on coastal and Baltic Sea colliers and at the time of his enlistment was a mate on one of the colliers owned by Mr. Walker of Whitby. Since then he had spent thirteen years in the navy, been promoted to boatswain and then to master. He had shown extraordinary skill in the charting of unknown coasts and waters, beginning with work in the St. Lawrence River in connection with General Wolfe's siege of Quebec.

A letter in the Admiralty files from Lord Colville,

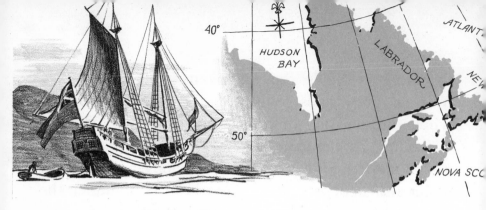

The Grenville

under whose command Cook had charted the Nova Scotia coast, informed their lordships "that from my experience of Mr. Cook's genius and capacity, I think him well qualified for the work he has performed and for greater undertakings of the same kind."

Captain Hugh Palliser, under whom Cook had also served in the navy, recommended him strongly. Palliser was now Governor of Newfoundland and it was at his request that Cook had been assigned for the last few years to survey the Newfoundland coast. For this work he commanded a schooner of his own, the *Grenville*, even though he was only a noncommissioned officer. Palliser was in London at the time. So was Cook, whose surveying work could only be done during the summer months.

Cook's record was good and somewhat unusual. In Britain's caste-ridden Navy, officers almost always came from the aristocracy and had been educated in the best schools. Cook was the son of a farm laborer and had had the most meager schooling. Yet his seamanship and self-taught knowledge of navigation had won him the respect of all the officers under whom he

16

had sailed. His charts of Nova Scotia and the upper St. Lawrence had been published by the Admiralty, and the Royal Society had published observations of an eclipse of the sun he had made in Newfoundland in 1766. Early in May Cook was introduced to the Council of the Royal Society and won their approval.

On May 25, 1768, James Cook, age forty, was summoned to the Admiralty and informed that he was to be commissioned a lieutenant and put in command of a ship going around the world. He was going to be a representative of the Royal Society and of the British government in the South Seas.

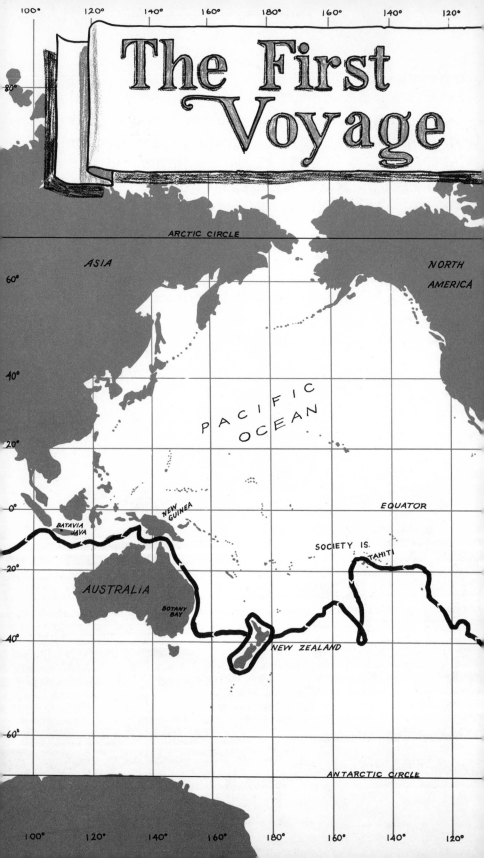

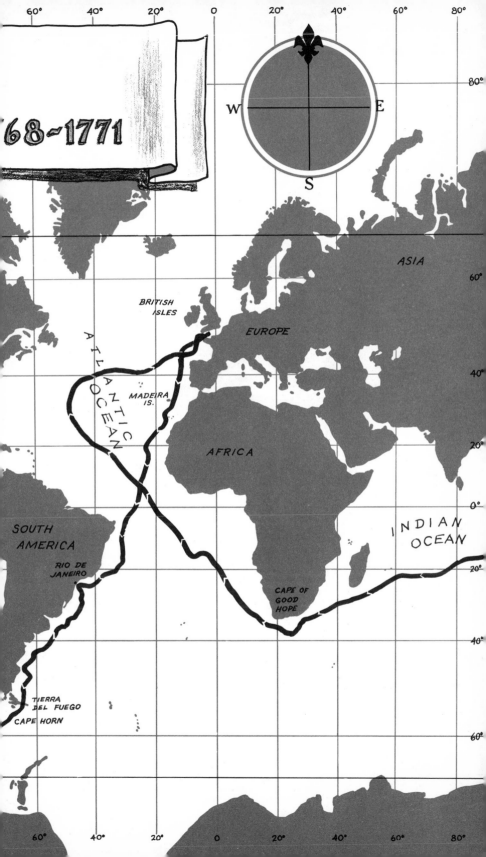

68~1771

W E

S

80°

60°

ASIA

BRITISH
ISLES

EUROPE

40°

ATLANTIC OCEAN

MADEIRA
IS.

20°

AFRICA

0°

INDIAN
OCEAN

SOUTH
AMERICA

RIO DE
JANEIRO

20°

CAPE OF
GOOD
HOPE

40°

TIERRA
DEL FUEGO

CAPE HORN

60°

The *Endeavour*

First Voyage: 1768–1771
New Jewels for the British Crown

Two days after his appointment, Lieutenant Cook went to the navy dockyard at Deptford to take command of his ship, the bark *Endeavour*. He was delighted with the vessel. It was a collier, built exactly like the

Walker ships on which he had served his apprenticeship.

The clumsy, slow ship, only 105 feet long, didn't look much like a man-of-war, but Cook knew it was especially good for surveying and exploring. A shallow-draft ship like this was ideal for approaching unknown lands and charting new coasts. It could easily be beached for repairs and could carry enough provisions for a long voyage.

Shortly after Cook began his preparations for the voyage the Admiralty sent over the crew list of seventy-two officers and men. Cook was highly pleased with his experienced crew. Lieutenant Gore had been around the world twice. The Master, Robert Molyneux, had just returned with Wallis from a voyage around the world. Five others had sailed around it once. And there were five hands from Cook's Newfoundland schooner, the *Grenville.*

Then a letter came from the Admiralty. It informed Cook that the Royal Society had appointed Mr. Charles Green to join him in observing the transit of Venus. It also told him of the Society's request that "for the advancement of useful knowledge" he take on board his ship "Joseph Banks, Esq., Fellow of that Society, a gentleman of large fortune, well versed in natural history . . . together with his suite and their baggage." Mr. Bank's "suite" consisted of eight persons. They included a highly trained botanist, Dr. Daniel Solander, favorite pupil of the great Swedish scientist Linnaeus; two artists to draw the plants they would collect; and four servants.

Arrival of the Banks party

At the end of July, refitted and with its stores loaded, the *Endeavour* sailed down the Thames to the great naval base at Plymouth, where the Banks party and a complement of twelve marines would board her. There Cook received his official *Instructions* from the Admiralty. He was ordered to proceed by way of Cape Horn to King George's Island (Tahiti) and observe the transit of Venus there in June, 1769. Then, the closing sentence read, "When this service is performed, you are to put to sea without loss of time, and carry into execution the Additional Instructions contained in the enclosed sealed packet."

Cook turned over in his hands the packet marked SECRET and read: "To be opened only after other Instructions have been fulfilled." He put the sealed envelope away in a trunk and locked it up. Clearly, this was not only a scientific voyage but one of exploration as well, designed to do more than observe Venus and collect plants. It was secret because England did not want it known abroad that it had a ship in the South Pacific searching for the supposed continent. Cook would have to wait a whole year to find out just where he was to go.

On Friday, August 26th, in a light breeze, the *Endeavour* glided out of Plymouth Harbor for Tahiti and places unknown. On board were ninety-four persons, including officers, seamen, marines, gentlemen and their servants.

After stops at the island of Madeira, Rio de Janeiro, and Tierra del Fuego, the *Endeavour* set out to round Cape Horn. In thirty-three days they were safely in the Pacific. Cook was not satisfied, however, with just getting there. He mapped everything possible on the way. His charts were different from all previous ones. As he explained it, "I have laid down no land nor figure'd out any shore but what I saw myself, and thus far the Chart may be depended upon." The charts he had

Leaving Plymouth Harbor

brought along for the voyage were wrong both in their shore lines and in latitude and longitude measurements. But the ones Cook drew were completely trustworthy. "I can now venture to assert," he wrote in his journal, "that the Longitude of few parts of the World are better ascertained than that of Cape Horn." A new era of scientific navigation had begun as the *Endeavour* sailed westward into the Pacific.

After leaving Tierra del Fuego, the *Endeavour* did not touch land for over two and a half months. Even though they had already been at sea for five months, there was no sign of scurvy on board and all hands were in good health. This was an extraordinary record.

Toward the end of a ship's third month out of port scurvy usually started to show itself. The crew would begin to feel listless and lazy. Their skin would turn pale and spotty. Then their gums would swell and rot until their teeth fell out. Pains began in arms and legs. Scars of old wounds opened up as if they had never healed. Men would faint at the least exertion. Scurvy victims who tried to work often dropped dead while performing their tasks. Ships sometimes became such floating hospitals that there were not enough able men to furl the sails or drop the anchor.

Cook was determined that this voyage was not going to fail because of scurvy. With the cooperation of the Admiralty, he had had ten tons of sauerkraut and other antiscurvy foods put into the holds. His big problem was to get the seamen to eat sauerkraut, as it was totally unfamiliar to English sailors. He did this by serving it to the officers and persuading them to eat it, while the seamen could take it or leave it as they chose. By the time a week was out Cook found it necessary to put everyone on board on an allowance. If a man showed the slightest symptoms of the disease he was immediately put in the care of the surgeon, who had other remedies, including a special malt preparation and condensed lemon juice. Even though no one

knew at the time that scurvy was caused by the lack of Vitamin C, it was known that certain foods could prevent the disease. Besides the antiscurvy foods taken along from England, Cook always made it a rule to collect as much fresh green food as possible at any land they touched.

Cook also tightened old rules and made new ones for the health of his crew. The system of watches was changed so that all hands had longer periods to rest, warm up, and get wet clothes dried out. He kept a fire burning at the bottom of the well in the hold to circulate air and keep the quarters dry. Decks were fumigated weekly and both quarters and clothing were kept spotlessly clean.

Paradise in Tahiti

At seven o'clock on the morning of April 13, the *Endeavour* dropped anchor in the beautiful harbor of Royal Bay, Tahiti. All hands on board had their eyes glued on this South Sea Island paradise that Commander Wallis had discovered only two years before. Around them rose a mountainous, green land surrounded by a green lagoon. Chains of waterfalls spilled from high, wild, craggy peaks. Just before them was a beach of sand fringed with beautiful palm trees.

27

Cook stood in full uniform in the blazing sun, surrounded by his officers and the scientific gentlemen. They watched as brown Tahitians jumped into canoes and paddled out to the big ship. Breadfruit, coconuts, and other products of the island were piled high in the canoes. Lieutenant Gore, who had been with Wallis, recognized old friends and introduced them to Cook. Gifts were exchanged and the Englishmen were delighted by the greetings of these charming people.

Before anyone was allowed to go on shore, Cook read his officers and men a solemn order: "All are to try to be friendly with the natives and treat them with humanity."

During the following days the officers and crew made friends with the Tahitians and much trading was

done for the produce of the island—breadfruit, coconuts, bananas, plaintains, sweet potatoes, yams, and
other fruits and vegetables. There were clams, lobsters,
crabs, and fish from the sea, as well as hogs and chick-
ens from the land. All of these were exchanged for
things precious to the Tahitians—nails and cloth from
the ship.

But the main job was to find a good spot on shore
where the instruments could be set up to observe the
transit of Venus. A suitable location was selected on the
sandy shore, and permission was secured from the
chiefs to occupy it for six weeks. Tents were set up and
a real fort built to protect the observers and the precious instruments they needed. Cook wanted to be

The Fort

prepared in case any trouble with the people should develop. The great source of danger was the Tahitians' constant thieving. On the *Endeavour* it was hard to keep them from carrying off everything loose. On shore the English had to keep a sharp watch. Spyglasses, snuff boxes, pistols, disappeared from their pockets, stockings and coats from under their pillows while they slept. Anything could be snatched from anywhere by these wonderful, friendly, skillful, and peaceful people. They stole with an ease, Cook observed, that "puts to shame the best pickpockets in Europe." It was not malicious. They simply saw no reason whatever why they shouldn't appropriate any of the strange and fascinating things the foreigners possessed. Even a quadrant, indispensable for the observation of Venus, but utterly useless to the islanders, was carried off in its heavy packing case from under the nose of a sentry. After an all-day search the quadrant was recovered.

All the while, the officers, gentlemen, and all hands on the *Endeavour* were having the time of their lives on this beautiful island. In spite of the constant thieving, the Englishmen came to admire the people.

The men were tall and handsome; the women were lovely. All of them were graceful, gracious, and exceedingly clean, bathing three times a day, morning, noon, and night, in the deep clear water of rivers that ran down to the sea. They were an easygoing and gentle people who cared greatly for the pleasures of each day and gave little thought to the future. Nature was bountiful and, as Cook observed, they were exempt from the biblical curse that man must get his living by the sweat of his brow.

June 3 was the day of the transit of Venus. Cook was out of his shore tent in the fort at daybreak. There was not a cloud in the sky and the air was perfectly clear. Patiently and with great excitement, Cook, Green, and Solander watched, each with his own telescope, while the planet Venus passed across the face of the broiling sun. Two other parties that had been sent in boats to neighboring islands observed it too.

Cook had now completed his duties under the public instructions. The transit of Venus had been observed and the time Venus reached the sun's disc and left it duly recorded. That night, back in his cabin aboard ship, he unlocked the trunk and took out the sealed packet from the Admiralty.

The document stated that it would be to the honor of Britain, and her trade would be increased, if countries then unknown should be discovered or others, poorly explored, mapped. The Admiralty wanted Cook to find out if there was a great southern continent. He was therefore to sail south to the latitude of 40°. If he didn't see signs of any such continent he was then to sail west till he either reached it or New Zealand. If he discovered a new continent he was to note its position and chart its coast.

Then came an instruction Cook had never had before. If he found a country uninhabited, he was to take possession of it for His Majesty by setting up proper marks as its first discoverer.

The *Endeavour* was quickly loaded with fruit and fresh meat and made ready to leave. Every day before their departure, a few Tahitians volunteered to go with

16°20'

MAUPITI

them. One of these was Tupia, a chief and priest who had spent a great deal of time with the Englishmen. Cook decided he was the best one to take along. He recognized Tupia's intelligence and was struck by his knowledge of the stars, of the geography of the surrounding islands, and of the laws and customs of their people. And so Tupia, and a young boy who was his servant, sailed with the *Endeavour* when she left Tahiti, July 13, 1769.

With Tupia's expert help, Cook explored the neighboring islands. He named the whole group the "Society Islands" in honor of the Royal Society. On August 15th he sailed to the south, in accordance with his instructions.

Early in September they reached latitude 40° 22'

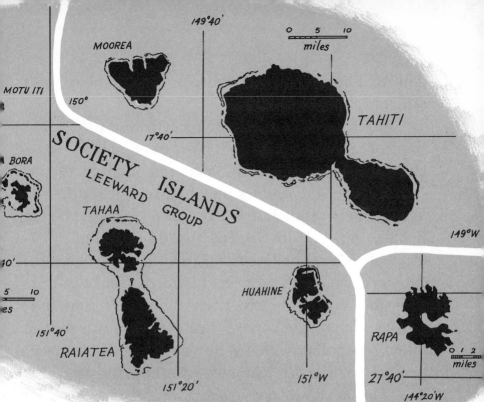

South without sighting land. From studying all known charts, Cook was certain that no one had ever sailed in these waters. He wanted to continue farther south, but the gales were too violent. At this point he ordered the course changed to the northwest. That way lay the unexplored and unmapped land of New Zealand.

Exploring New Zealand

The Dutch navigator Abel Tasman had discovered New Zealand in 1642, but he had not been able to land on it because of fierce attacks by the native New Zealanders. No European had seen its coasts since. Was this a coast of the great unknown southern continent? Banks and some of the officers were sure it was. Cook had

35

doubts. The only way to find out, he told them, was to sail completely around it.

After a month of sailing northwest they caught sight of land on October 7. Two days later Cook had himself rowed ashore with Banks and Solander to speak with some of the natives they had seen from the ship. When they landed, the "Indians" (they called all peoples in the South Sea Indians) disappeared. Then a few stole out of the forest and tried to capture the boat from which Cook's party had landed. Guns were fired over the natives' heads. Even this didn't stop them. They left only when one of their members was shot and killed by another volley of muskets. This did not promise well for friendly relations with these people.

The next two days were worse, even with Tupia speaking to the New Zealanders in his Tahitian tongue, which they understood perfectly. Fights started upon each attempt to establish relations, and ended with one or more Zealanders being killed. Cook was sick at heart and troubled at having to order shooting. He did not want to fight these people, whose courage he greatly admired and who were so helpless against British guns. There was no alternative but to sail away and try landing somewhere else.

Two days later Cook sailed out of what he named *Poverty Bay* because it afforded them nothing they wanted. Some distance north they sailed into the Bay of Islands, past the site of the present city of Auckland. There were Maori villages on the mainland and on the islands. Every day four or five hundred Maori warriors

36

came alongside them in their large canoes. Great ugly faces were carved on the prows of the canoes with large eyes of mother-of-pearl and tongues sticking out toward the sea. The warriors were well built and strong. Cook

had learned how courageous they were. In this thickly populated area he had to be very careful. Any incident that made these people hostile could be dangerous. One such soon occurred when a group of Maoris tried to pull up their anchor. Cook again avoided a real battle with the New Zealanders. But was there anywhere in all this land he could safely stay awhile and replenish his supplies?

The *Endeavour* sailed out of the Bay of Islands and headed north. They rounded the northernmost point of New Zealand and Cook named it *North Cape.* Then they sailed down the western coast. By mid-January they reached a beautiful bay which Cook named *Queen Charlotte's Sound,* after the wife of George III. They found the natives mildly friendly. Here, at last, they could drop anchor, explore the shores, fill their water casks, and gather wild celery and grasses as safeguards against scurvy. The Maoris were ready to trade with them. The *Endeavour* crew soon found, however, that they were cannibals.

One day, while walking in the beautiful forest and listening to the wild melodies of many strange birds, the crew came upon a grizzly scene. A group of Maoris had just finished feasting on human flesh. Cook examined a man's forearm with the flesh still on it.

Through Tupia, Cook asked, "Have you eaten the flesh of a man?"

The answer was, "Yes." Then the Maoris told them how a few days before they had captured, killed, and eaten a canoe's crew of seven of their enemies.

Cook felt his job was not to judge but to observe and try to understand the customs of the people he encountered. He felt they were lucky to have met with cannibalism and lived to tell the tale.

The time spent in Queen Charlotte's Sound was full of activity. A camp was established on shore. Casks of water were hauled on board. Timber was cut from the rich forests surrounding them for repairs and firewood. The ship was caulked and seamed. Sails were repaired.

The big question in Cook's mind was whether there was a passage from Queen Charlotte's Sound

through to the eastern coast. If there was, then New Zealand was not one island but two or more. One day he climbed to the top of a hill and saw enough of a passage to convince him "that there is the greatest probability in the world of its running into the eastern sea." He returned in high spirits to the ship, where he reported his discovery to the others. They would proceed, he said, to sail the *Endeavour* through the strait, as soon as they could put up the proper marker and the British flag to claim these lands for King George.

Early in February 1770, they started to sail through the passage which Banks insisted be named *Cook Strait*. When safely through the dangerous passage and in the open ocean, a new argument arose. Some of the officers argued that northern New Zealand might be connected with the great southern continent between Cook Strait and a cape farther north where they had

41

turned about earlier. Cook was sure they were wrong, but to convince them he sailed north. Two days later they sighted the familiar cape. It was evident to all that they had now sailed around an island. They turned about to head south, and Cook named the point Cape *Turnagain.*

They sailed on past Cook Strait down the coast of the south island of New Zealand. They rounded the southern point and headed north toward Queen Char-

lotte's Sound, charting the coast as they went. Finally they completed the circumnavigation of New Zealand.

Cook was now free, under his instructions, to sail back to England by any route he chose. Saturday night, March 31, 1770, he held a conference with his officers, proposing the return by Cape Horn to explore more of the Pacific. The officers protested that they had insufficient provisions and that the ship, sails, and rigging were not fit for such an undertaking in the southern winter that was approaching. Cook then proposed they sail for the east coast of New Holland, as Australia was then called. No one had ever been on that coast. They would follow it to the north and then return to England by way of the East Indies and the Cape of Good Hope. All agreed.

At daybreak on Sunday, April 1st, the *Endeavour* headed for Australia.

That night Cook finished his journal on New Zealand. He was proud and happy at claiming this great land for his king, his country, and his countrymen. It was as big as the British Isles themselves. It was a rich and fertile land, and he believed all sorts of European food plants and animals would thrive there. Its coasts were abundant with the tastiest fish, lobsters, and oysters. There was excellent timber. Cook reported that this was an extraordinarily good land for English settlements. Even the warlike Maoris, he wrote, could be won over by "kind and gentle usage."

Now he was on his way to explore another great land.

Australia and Near Shipwreck

After steering west for eighteen days the *Endeavour* sighted Australia. Cook finally found a safe anchorage in a bay south of the present city of Sydney. They had to get ashore for food and water. All wondered what the people were like. Would they greet them like the gracious Tahitians, or fight them like the Maori warriors of New Zealand? It turned out that the Australians were very different from both these peoples. Cook could not establish relations with them at all. Either they ran away when Cook and his party approached, or they tried to attack them with darts. Most of the time they simply ignored the Englishmen's presence. But every once in a while Cook caught glimpses of these tall dark-brown people, who wore no clothing of any kind. Then he would try to approach them, alone and unarmed, but they walked away into the woods.

After a week in *Botany Bay,* as Cook named it because Banks and Solander found it rich in new botanical specimens, they sailed north. For five weeks they went along Australia's east coast, naming hills and bays as they passed them. Then, without warning, they entered the dangerous waters between the Great Barrier Reef and the coast. The reef was a thousand-mile-long coral ridge that paralleled the coast and then curved in closer and closer to it the farther north it went. Cook was in a trap and did not know it.

One beautiful moonlit night they were sailing

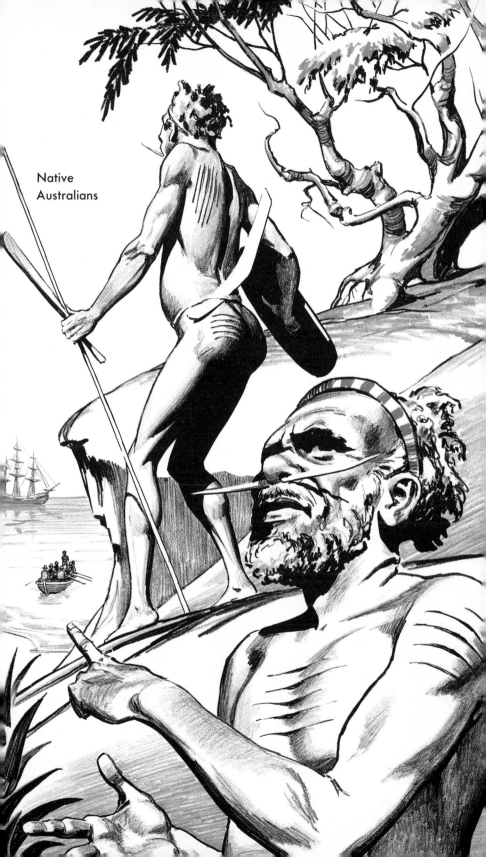

Native Australians

along with a fine breeze. The lead man was taking soundings of the depth. It was varying dangerously. Cook summoned everybody to their stations. At a few minutes before eleven the lead man called out, "Seventeen fathoms!" And before he could throw the lead out again for another sounding, the ship struck bottom. It shivered, groaned, and stuck tight.

They were held fast on the edge of a coral reef. No maneuvers budged the ship. The worst of it was that it was high tide. There was little chance of floating off. All that night every hand was engaged in lightening the ship. They threw overboard everything that could possibly be moved and spared. The cannon, the water casks, the wormy bisquits, the ballast—forty to fifty tons of their stores—went over the side. Even so, at the next high tide in midmorning, the ship couldn't be moved an inch. She started to lean to starboard. Water was pouring into her hold. As the hours passed the leak increased. Suddenly, after the most desperate measures,

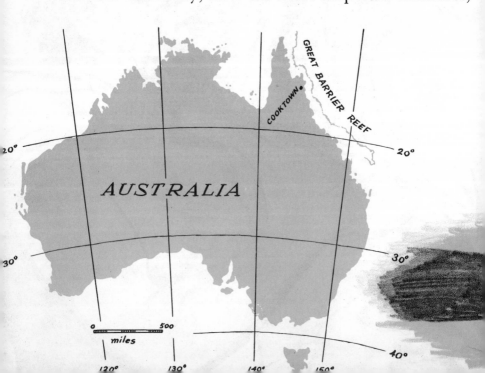

the *Endeavour* floated off. They were free, but the ship was leaking nearly as fast as all hands could pump. They pulled a sail covered with oakum under the ship to cover the biggest hole. This stopped the leak enough for them to try to get to shore.

Ninety lives were at stake. The results of all their discoveries were in danger. Cook resolved that he would never again make such a voyage in unknown waters without two ships. Banks was most impressed by Cook's behavior during this ordeal. Without food or sleep for twenty-four hours, he remained perfectly calm and fearless, giving orders quietly and radiating confidence to everyone on board. Cook, on the other hand, wrote in his journal: "In justice to the ship's company, I must say that no men ever behaved better than they have done on this occasion." And he praised the gentlemen on board, too, for setting a perfect example.

They sailed for the nearest point on the coast and beached the ship on the shore of an inlet they named *Endeavour River*—now the site of Cooktown. The damage was frightening. Planks had been cut out of the hull as if with a giant knife. If a large piece of coral rock had not been wedged into one great hole they could never have kept the ship from sinking. It took over a month to repair the leak.

Meanwhile the officers and gentlemen explored the countryside. Boat crews went out to catch turtles. Others seined in the river mouth. Wild beans were collected along the sandy beaches, and a vegetable growing in the bogs tasted better than English spinach. The few sick quickly recovered, and the crew as a whole became healthy and strong. Turtles, fresh fish, greens—everything that was found—was distributed

equally among the whole company. Neither Cook nor
the aristocratic Banks got more of the antiscurvy foods
than the humblest person on board. Cook believed this
a rule "every commander of a ship on such a voyage as
this ought ever to observe."

Some of the company saw signs of a strange animal. It was the size of a deer and the color of a mouse.
But it seemed to leap instead of run. Finally, Lieutenant Gore shot one and dragged it back to the beached
ship. The scientists were excited by this new animal and
studied it carefully. They learned from some natives
thereabouts that it was called *kangaroo*.

Finally, the *Endeavour* was patched up enough to
sail. At five o'clock on the morning of August 4 they set

out for Batavia on the island of Java. If they could make this great Dutch port they could get the ship fully repaired, buy new sails and ropes, and everything else needed for the final journey around the Cape of Good Hope to England.

The second day out from Endeavour River, Cook became uneasy. They were surrounded by banks and shoals, and a strong wind prevented their going back the way they had come. Was there a passage inside the Great Barrier Reef? No one knew, for no one had ever sailed in these waters before.

By day they inched along northeast, always with a boat ahead to take soundings. When darkness came they anchored. At night they were fairly safe, but it was a daytime nightmare for eight days. Finally Cook decided to make a break for open water. There seemed to be a possible channel among the dangerous coral islands. With one of their boats in the lead and the help of a strong tide, Cook got the *Endeavour* out of the reefs and into open sea again.

Three days later they found themselves being blown into a great line of breakers between them and the coast. They tried everything. They tacked one way, then the other. The surf was roaring near them, yet the water was too deep for their anchor to hold. When the wind stopped and their sails were useless a strong current carried them toward the reef. Cook and his officers believed it was hopeless. Then they saw a possible opening, not even a hundred feet wide. It was their only chance. They maneuvered the ship into position and a flood tide carried them through. Cook named it *Providential Channel* and properly located it on his accurate and growing chart of the Great Barrier Reef.

Now they were in the same quiet water they had been so happy to escape from a few days earlier. Creeping north inside the reef, they soon reached the northeast point of Australia. Cook landed and on August 22 took possession of eastern Australia for the British crown. He called it *New South Wales*. Since leaving Tahiti he had charted over 5000 miles of unknown coast lines and claimed two great lands for his country.

Now they had one task—to get to Batavia as soon as possible. Then, with repairs and supplies, they could sail back to England. The trip was uneventful,

but when they arrived at Batavia the damage to the *Endeavour* was found to be even greater than they had dreamed. The Dutch shipworkers were surprised that they had been able to keep her above water at all.

Disaster at Batavia

It took two and a half months to get the *Endeavour* into shape. Cook used the early weeks to correct his journal and copy his charts, which he sent home to the Admiralty by a Dutch packet ship. He sent along a letter explaining it was not his fault that he did not discover the much-talked-of southern continent. It just wasn't to be found in any sea he had sailed. "My discoveries," he wrote, "are not great, yet I flatter myself they are such as may merit the attention of their Lordships." The last statement in his long letter read, "I have the satisfaction to say that I have not lost one man by sickness during the whole Voyage."

This letter was written on October 23, 1770. Cook did not know then that the next two months in Batavia during the rainy season would result in an epidemic of malaria and dysentery among his men. Tupia and his servant from Tahiti, Surgeon Monkhouse, Mr. Green's servant, and three seamen, died on shore. And most of the others became terribly ill.

The day after Christmas a sad crew returned on board. It was a hospital ship that sailed for the Cape of Good Hope and England. More than forty were sick, and most of the rest, including Cook, were in a weakened condition. The next six weeks were a horror. First Lieutenant Hicks died; then Molyneux the master; then the astronomer Green, and Parkinson the artist. Twenty-three others of the crew and the Royal Society

party had to be buried in the water overside the *Endeavour*.

At one stage in this dreadful voyage only twelve men on board could attend to their duties. Cook was desolate. His valiant fight against scurvy had succeeded beyond any possible expectation. But what was it all worth when nearly half of his people died from diseases contracted in a so-called "civilized" port? "What causes them?" Cook asked. His only answer was: "Some way must be found to prevent them, for both the good of seamen and mankind in general."

On July 13, 1771, the *Endeavour* finally anchored in the English channel, nearly three years after it had set sail.

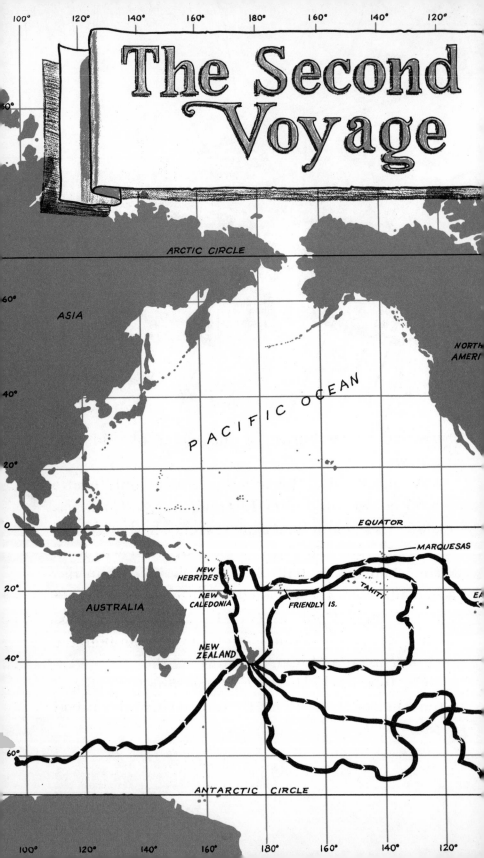

The Second Voyage

100° 120° 140° 160° 180° 160° 140° 120°

ARCTIC CIRCLE

60°

ASIA

NORTH AMERI

40°

PACIFIC OCEAN

20°

0 EQUATOR

MARQUESAS

NEW HEBRIDES

NEW CALEDONIA

20° TAHITI

FRIENDLY IS. EA

AUSTRALIA

NEW ZEALAND

40°

60°

ANTARCTIC CIRCLE

100° 120° 140° 160° 180° 160° 140° 120°

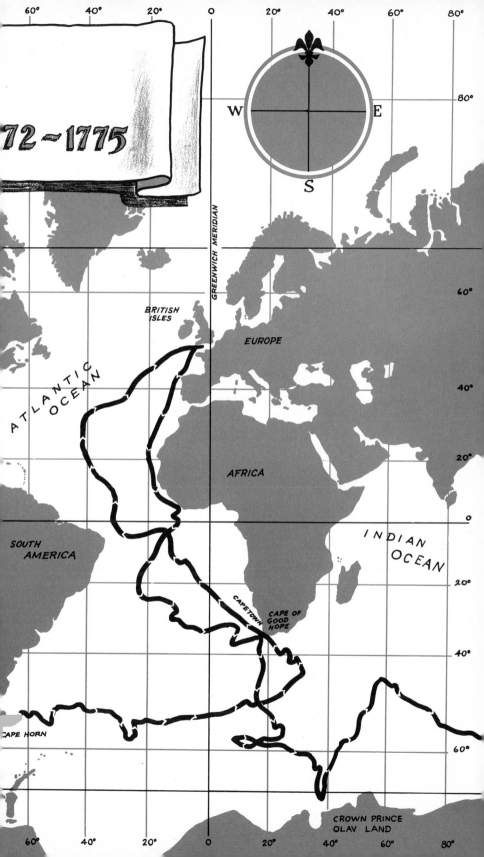

Second Voyage: 1772–1775
There Is No Southern Continent

Cook found himself famous. The Dutch ship had delivered his papers to the Admiralty months before and his achievements had become widely known. King George III summoned him to Buckingham Palace and ordered him appointed a commander. He was invited to dinner at the house of the new First Lord of the Admiralty, Lord Sandwich—the man whose name is known to everyone for his invention of putting food between two slices of bread. Cook was also entertained at other dinners, where he met the leading writers and painters of the day. James Cook, son of a farm laborer, had become one of England's great men.

Joseph Banks and Dr. Solander had achieved fame too. They brought back one of the first botanical collections ever made in the Pacific islands—a thousand plants never before described by any botanists. They had collected, described, and had their artists draw some five hundred birds and fish, too, not to mention countless insects. For a century to come it was almost routine for a British naval ship going around the world to take along a naturalist. It was in this tradition that Captain Robert Fitzroy took the young Charles Darwin on the *Beagle's* voyage in the 1830's.

Before long there began to be talk of a second voyage. There was still the possibility of a southern continent. Dalrymple admitted that Cook had shown it didn't exist in the western Pacific. Then it must be in the eastern Pacific! He drew a map showing a southern continent with boundaries that extended anywhere and everywhere Cook had not been. The Admiralty knew that if there were such a continent, the nation that discovered it would be the greatest power on earth. If there were no such continent, the sooner England found it out the better.

In the fall of 1771, Cook was appointed to command a new expedition. It was to sail from the Cape of Good Hope as far south as it could, then east around the world in higher latitudes than any ship had ever done. This should settle the question of a southern continent once and for all.

Cook insisted on two ships so that all would not be lost if one were wrecked. They had to be Whitby colliers, too. Cook believed them almost a necessity on voyages of this kind. No other type of vessel could possibly have survived what the *Endeavour* did on the Great Barrier Reef.

One ship, the *Adventure*, was put in command of Captain Furneaux, who had sailed around the world with Wallis. Cook's ship was the *Resolution*, a vessel of 462 tons that was to carry a total crew of 110. The smaller *Adventure* would carry eighty-two men.

Both ships were generously equipped. Cook's old friend and patron, Sir Hugh Palliser, now an admiral, was comptroller of the Navy. He saw to it that Cook was provided with everything he wanted in the way of food, clothing, and other stores. The crews were carefully selected. Many of the officers of the *Endeavour* signed on again. John Reinhold Forster was hired as the naturalist for the voyage. He took along his seventeen-year-old son George as his assistant.

In addition to the Forsters, the Admiralty hired two astronomers, one for each ship. This was something new in navigation. The Admiralty was determined to conquer the problem of longitude, or how to determine

the east-west position at any point on the earth. Measuring latitude, or the distance north and south of the Equator, was easy. You needed only to know the day of the year and have at hand charts of the sun's position

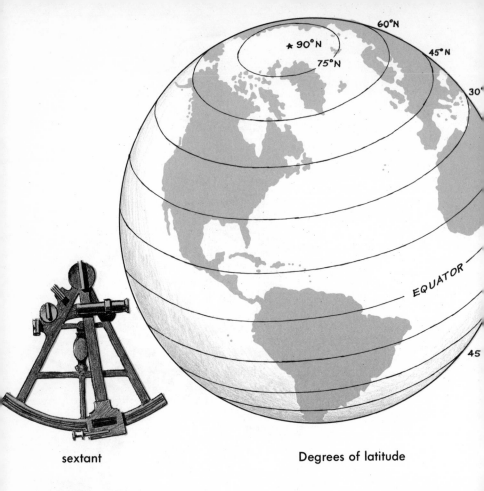

sextant

Degrees of latitude

for each day. Then, with an instrument called a sextant, a trained person could measure the angle between the sun and the horizon and get the latitude.

But determining longitude was quite another thing. It was such a serious problem that every maritime nation had offered prizes for a simple and reliable method of finding longitude on distant sea voyages.

The great scientist Isaac Newton had offered the answer in theory. The earth is a sphere and like all spheres is conventionally divided into 360°. It turns on its axis every 24 hours. Each hour is therefore equiva-

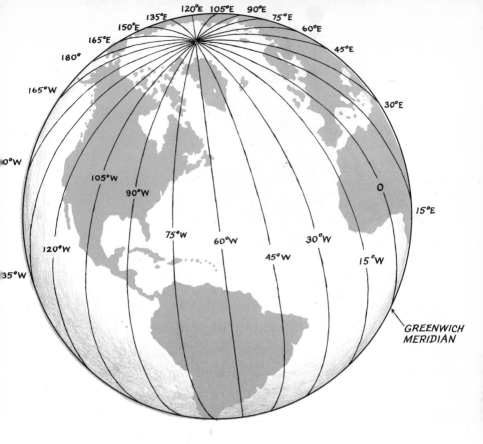

Degrees of longitude

lent to 15° of longitude (360 ÷ 24). With two clocks, one keeping time as it is at any definite point on the earth's surface (Greenwich, England became the accepted point) and the other kept on local ship time by observation of the sun and stars, you could easily determine your longitude at any time. If time on shipboard, for example, was just four hours later than Greenwich time, the ship's longitude would be 4 × 15 or 60° east of Greenwich. In this way the difference between the two clocks would give the east-west position anywhere on earth.

63

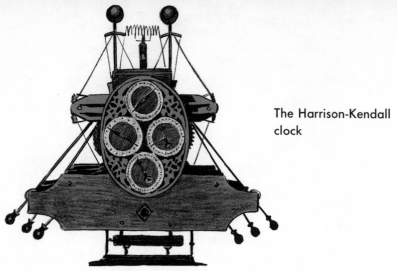

The Harrison-Kendall clock

The trouble was that no clock had yet been made that could keep accurate time on a long ocean voyage. It had to be unaffected by the ship's rolling and changes in temperature. These were difficult things to offset.

Way back in 1714, the British Parliament had offered a prize of £20,000 (about $100,000) for a clock that would keep accurate time at sea. A British clock-maker, John Harrison, worked most of his life making several marine timekeepers. The fourth one he made was almost perfect. It was tested on a short voyage and found to be amazingly accurate. John Harrison got half the prize money. The Admiralty then spent thousands of dollars having this clock copied by an expert watchmaker, Larcum Kendall. It took him seventeen years to do it. Only recently finished, this chronometer, as these extremely accurate timepieces came to be called, was put on board the *Resolution*.

Three years later Cook reported to the Admiralty that it was "our never-failing guide." After three years at sea, it was only seven minutes and forty-five seconds off Greenwich time. Thus Cook's second voyage ushered in a new era in navigation. Cook could always know almost exactly where he was on the earth's surface, even after many months without seeing land. The same Harrison-Kendall clock is still running in the Royal Observatory at Greenwich.

Finally both ships were fully prepared in Plymouth Harbor. There were enough provisions for two whole years. There were plenty of foods that could prevent or cure scurvy. There was even a new distilling device that could make three gallons of fresh water out of sea water every hour.

On July 13, 1772, the two ships sailed out of Plymouth for Cape Town. This time there were no secret instructions. There were really no "instructions" at all, for Cook himself proposed the plan of this voyage to the Admiralty.

October 30 they reached Cape Town. Cook noted that not one of the nearly two hundred men on board the two ships was on the sick list. Yet they had been sailing for three and a half months. It was clear to him that scurvy could be beaten.

But Cook knew that the time they had been out at sea was nothing compared to what lay ahead. He sent his crews on shore, a dozen at a time, to refresh themselves. He saw that each man got freshly baked bread and fresh beef or mutton every day. He had the men served as many green vegetables as he could get them to eat. Cook was not only exploring the southern ocean; he was also pioneering in preventive medicine.

Into the Antarctic

Then the real voyage began. They set sail from the Cape of Good Hope, heading south to where no ships had ever gone. The voyage was timed to get them toward the Antarctic in its midsummer, which is the Northern Hemisphere's midwinter.

On November 24, Cook ordered special warm clothing distributed. It was getting colder daily. December 12, the thermometer dropped below freezing. They sailed past huge icebergs. The biggest ones were two miles around and two hundred feet high. Whales played about the two ships. Penguins dived into the water from their perches on the floating ice. Great white birds, the albatrosses, circled the ships.

On December 14 they were stopped by an immense ice field. Cook dropped his sails, hove to, and sent a boat for Captain Furneaux. There was danger of their being separated amidst these icebergs, and they needed to set a rendezvous. They were now 55° South and 22° East of Greenwich. Before the Antarctic winter set in they could sail in that general latitude clear around to near 180° East. Then they would head north to New Zealand and Queen Charlotte's Sound. There they could get fresh food and good water among not-unfriendly natives.

For nearly two months the two ships kept within sight or signaling distance of each other. Fog and snow surrounded them. The rigging and sails glittered with icicles. There were huge floating mountains of ice on the north and a field of ice on the south. This threatened constantly to freeze them fast and hold them for months on end.

Was there land beyond the ice fields? Cook was sure there was, for two reasons. First, he was certain that the great mountains of ice he saw couldn't have come from the sea itself. Second, he found that the loose ice around them was frozen fresh water. It came, therefore, from frozen snow and not frozen ocean. In a

few hours, shortly after Christmas, three boats gathered
enough ice to yield fifteen tons of good fresh water. This
was a most fortunate discovery. The guard could now
be removed from the water casks.

On January 17 they crossed the Antarctic Circle,
the first ship that ever crossed that line. Thanks to their

accurate instruments and skill in using them, Cook was able to record that at noon they were exactly four and a half miles inside the south polar circle. He was little more than 150 miles from what is now known as Crown Prince Olav Land in Antarctica.

The next morning he climbed to the masthead to see for himself what lay before them. As far as he could see, there was nothing but ice south, east, or west of them. He came down from his perch and held a brief conference with his officers. It was too risky to continue farther south, all agreed. They changed their course to the northeast.

On the ninth of February the two ships were separated in a thick fog. Cook fired a cannon and returned, by agreement with Furneaux, to where they had last seen the *Adventure*. For two days they cruised in the vicinity, without a sign of their companion ship. Cook then ordered the search given up. If all went well, they would meet again in the spring at the appointed anchorage in Queen Charlotte's Sound.

The *Resolution* sailed on alone. At night they wished for daylight so they could keep their eyes on the floating mountains of ice around them. When daylight came, they almost wished for darkness again, for the scene was even more fearful than they could imagine it in the gloom of the short Antarctic summer night. Yet they found the gigantic icebergs magnificent to look at, though menacing.

Finally, on March 17, Cook ordered the ship's course straight north toward New Zealand. After four months in such high latitudes, amid great hardships and dangers, he thought it time to give his people rest and refreshment. Nine days later they sailed into Dusky Bay in the southwest corner of New Zealand.

Dusky Bay

They had been at sea 117 days since leaving Cape Town and had sailed eleven thousand miles without once seeing land.

They tied up in a little cove in the bay. After the ice floes of the Antarctic it was a pleasure to be able to moor their ship to a tree and use another tree, that grew horizontally out from the shore, as a natural gangway. The men fished, shot wild fowl, took on firewood and water, and brewed beer from the tender tops of spruce trees boiled with the malt and molasses they had on board. Cook may have learned about this cure for scurvy from the French explorer, Carteret, who learned it from the Canadian Indians. None of the crew had scurvy, but the animals they had carried from England had all the symptoms of this disease. A pair of goats and a pair of pigs were put ashore in the hope that they might eat the wild greens and be cured. The goats died, but the pigs survived and their wild descendants are still known today as "Captain Cooks."

Pleasant as this delightful "vacation" was, it had to be brought to an end. On May 18 they reached Queen Charlotte's Sound and found the *Adventure,* which had been there six weeks. The great satisfaction of rejoining their companion ship was tempered by Cook's discovery that twenty of its men were down with scurvy. Cook was angry. Furneaux clearly hadn't followed the prescribed diet. He hadn't even required his men to eat sauerkraut and the other antiscurvy foods as part of their daily ration.

The next morning at daylight, Cook went on shore himself in search of wild celery and water cress and other greens he knew grew there. By breakfast time he returned with a boatload of vegetables and gave strict orders that they were to be boiled with wheat or oatmeal for the crews of both ships.

Into Unknown Pacific Waters

Four o'clock in the morning of June 7, 1773, the two ships sailed out of the harbor for another long lap of their voyage of exploration. They were going east between 40° and 46° South—latitudes that had never before been explored—until they reached longitude 135° East. Then they would sail north to Tahiti.

Once out at sea, Cook sat down to bring his journal up to date. After describing his plans for the next leg of the voyage, he added some bitter reflections that were in his mind during this second stay at Queen Charlotte's Sound. What had they given the Maoris of New Zealand? Had contact with Europeans been of value to these people? Had it improved their life? "No," Cook concluded, answering his own questions. "We introduce among them wants and perhaps diseases which they never before knew and which only serve to disturb that happy calm they and their forefathers had enjoyed." And to make his point sharper, he added: "If anyone denies the truth of this assertion let him tell me what the natives of the whole extent of America have gained by the commerce they have had with Europeans." Cook was seriously concerned with the effect of the discovery of these lands on the people who inhabited them. He wanted to bring benefits and not disasters, physical or moral, to the peoples he met.

No land was discovered as the two ships sailed east from New Zealand. They kept below 40° South and had gone about 3000 miles, or halfway to South America, when another outbreak of scurvy on the *Adventure* made Cook decide to turn north to Tahiti. By the time he reached there he had removed the possibility of a continent in another huge area of the Pacific.

The two ships spent a month at Tahiti and other islands of the Society group. On September 18, 1773, they sailed west to find a group of islands that had not been seen by Europeans since they were discovered 130 years before. Cook named them the *Friendly Islands* because the people on them gave the visitors such a wonderfully warm welcome.

From the Friendly Islands they set their course once again for New Zealand. On the evening of Octo-

ber 24 they reached the eastern entrance of Cook Strait. But during the night the winds rose, and by morning a violent gale was blowing. For nine successive days and nights they were buffeted helplessly about, scarcely able to eat or sleep. When the gale subsided the *Adventure* was nowhere to be seen. The *Resolution* was in such bad shape that Cook took her through Cook Strait and anchored in Queen Charlotte's Sound for food and repairs. Nearly a month passed without a sign of the *Adventure*. Cook decided to go on without her.

Before setting sail Cook wrote a message for the *Adventure,* describing his planned course. He left it in a bottle under a tree by their anchoring cove. On the tree he carved the words *LOOK UNDERNEATH.* November 25 they went back through Cook Strait and spent a day along the coast, firing their biggest guns, with no response.

A few days later Captain Furneaux arrived with the *Adventure.* He found the message but knew it was too

late to try to follow Cook. After a stay for food and repairs he set out on his own for Cape Horn and then the Cape of Good Hope. He got back to England

LOOK UNDERNEATH

a whole year ahead of Cook and was the first commander ever to sail around the earth from west to east.

Cook spent December and January along the southern ice fields between New Zealand and South America. Twice he dipped down and crossed the Antarctic Circle, but was stopped both times by the ice. All on board suffered terribly from the cold and the snow. The sails froze until they became like sheets of metal. The rigging was decorated with icicles. The ropes were like steel cables, and froze in the blocks or pulleys. It took almost superhuman effort to get a topsail up or down. And all the while they struggled in terrible gales to avoid being wrecked against the great drifting islands of ice. Some of these were as high as their main-topgallant masthead—two hundred feet above the water.

Toward the south the ice rose higher and higher into great mountains. Was there an opening anywhere in this great wall of ice? When it was plain he couldn't go one inch farther south, Cook ordered a northern tack. They were at that moment about 350 miles inside the Antarctic Circle, in what is now called the Amundsen Sea, and within a hundred miles of the Thurston Peninsula on the Antarctic Continent. It was January 30, 1774. Cook gave their position as 71° 10′ South latitude and 106° 54′ West longitude. No ship had ever been anywhere near there before. None was ever to get there again until February 15, 1960, when a United States icebreaker, the *Glacier,* announced that it had reached and passed Cook's mark.

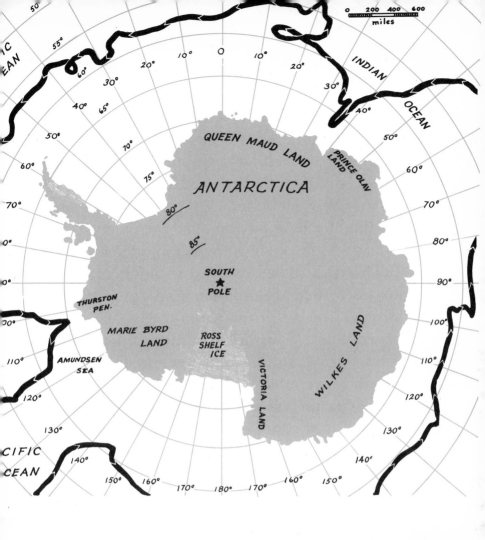

Even Cook admitted he was glad to be relieved "from the dangers and hardships of navigating these Southern Polar regions." That night he wrote in his journal, "I whose ambition leads me not only farther than any other man has been before me, but as far as I think it possible for man to go, was not sorry at meeting with this interruption."

They sailed north through a great area of the Pacific that was all but unknown. On March 11, 1774, they reached Easter Island, with its great stone statues that have made it famous. They sailed on to rediscover the Marquesas—which hadn't been visited since 1595 —to Tahiti, and then to the New Hebrides.

At the New Hebrides Cook repeated an act of courage that by now was familiar to his crew. They wanted badly to get on shore to cut wood and get fresh food. But hardly had they dropped anchor than islanders in canoes swarmed around them and onto the ship. A fight started and an arrow was aimed at Cook, who only saved himself by firing a musket loaded with small shot. Arrows and muskets were fired, and a four-pounder shot over their heads sent the canoeists off. But the war drums started to beat. The next morning Cook landed in the face of about five hundred people gathered on the shore, all armed with bows and arrows,

Easter
Island

clubs and spears. Cook advanced alone, holding a green branch in his hand. There was a moment of uncertainty. Then the chief gave his bow and arrows to another and walked toward Cook, also holding a green branch. When he reached Cook he exchanged branches with him, took him by the hand and led him up to the crowd. Immediately Cook distributed presents among them. His simple act of courage and dignity broke the ice, and friendly relations were established.

On the way back to New Zealand Cook discovered the large island of New Caledonia, that had somehow been missed by all previous explorers even though it was near beaten trails. He wanted to chart the whole coast

of this new land, but it was already September and the season for exploring in the Antarctic was approaching. He went on to New Zealand, and at Queen Charlotte's Sound found that the bottle left for the *Adventure* was gone. Nearby trees had been cut down. Captain Furneaux must have been there, but no message had been put in the place of the one Cook left. All breathed more easily, for at least the ship had not gone down in the terrible gale of the year before. It seemed clear that Furneaux, who was headed for England, never dreamed that Cook would be back here another year.

Then came a disquieting note. Some of the officers and gentlemen who went on shore heard strange stories from the neighboring Maoris about a ship that had been in the sound. The stories went that clothes were stolen from seamen ashore, that muskets were fired, Maoris shot dead and seamen killed with patoo-patoos (short flat clubs). Cook was worried. Was the *Adventure* lost here? Was all its crew killed? He tried questioning the natives himself, but the very ones who had first told the story now denied every word. Clearly, only time could clear up the mystery.

On November 11, 1774, the *Resolution,* with all sails set, started on its third successive voyage in high southern latitudes. Cook's plan was to cross the vast southern ocean from New Zealand to Cape Horn between 54° and 55° South latitude. This would show that no continent lay in this previously unexplored part of the South Pacific. On December 17 they sighted Tierra del Fuego and Cook wrote that he "was now

Passing Tierra del Fuego

done with the Southern Pacific Ocean." Twelve days later they rounded Cape Horn and entered the South Atlantic.

By February, Cook, like every man on board, was sick of the endless ice and thick fogs. He was now positive that there was no southern continent where the "dry land" school of geographers had put one. Dalrymple had complained that the first voyage hadn't disproved the existence of such a continent. It was obvious to him that it lay just where Cook hadn't been. But now Cook had covered the remaining areas, so that there was no place left for it to be—except within the Antarctic Circle. Cook was convinced there was a continent there. But this one, he was sure, was totally inaccessible.

On February 6 he entered into his journal one of his rare predictions. "I can be bold to say," he wrote, "that no man will ever venture farther than I have done and that the lands which may lie to the south

will never be explored." The continent that is likely
there is "doomed by nature to lie forever buried under
everlasting snow and ice." Its actual discovery, he concluded, would not be "of the least use either to navigation, geography or indeed any other science."

On March 21 they reached the Cape of Good
Hope. The crew was well but the ship was in dreadful
shape. For the first time they got word of the *Adventure*.
She had called there on her way back to London,
exactly one year before. They also heard the dreadful
story of how, when in Queen Charlotte's Sound, a
whole boat crew of ten men from the *Adventure* were
killed and eaten by the same Maoris Cook got along
so well with. This was the story they hadn't wanted to
tell him.

On July 29, 1775, the *Resolution* sighted land near
Plymouth, England. They had been at sea longer than
any previous ship in history. They had sailed about
70,000 miles, or a distance of nearly three times around

the earth. They had explored great unknown areas of the Pacific and had completely circumnavigated the south-polar world of ice. Four men had met their deaths on the trip, one from illness and three from accidents. None had died of scurvy. Mr. Forster, the scientist, who had so hated the hardships of the voyage and had no love for Cook or the British sailors, made some calculations. He figured that, from current death rates of men in England, it was two and a half times safer to sail with Cook than to stay at home.

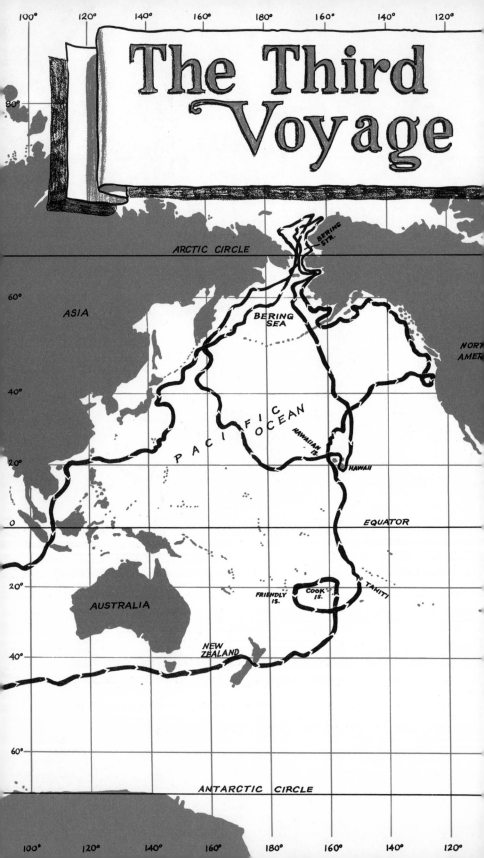

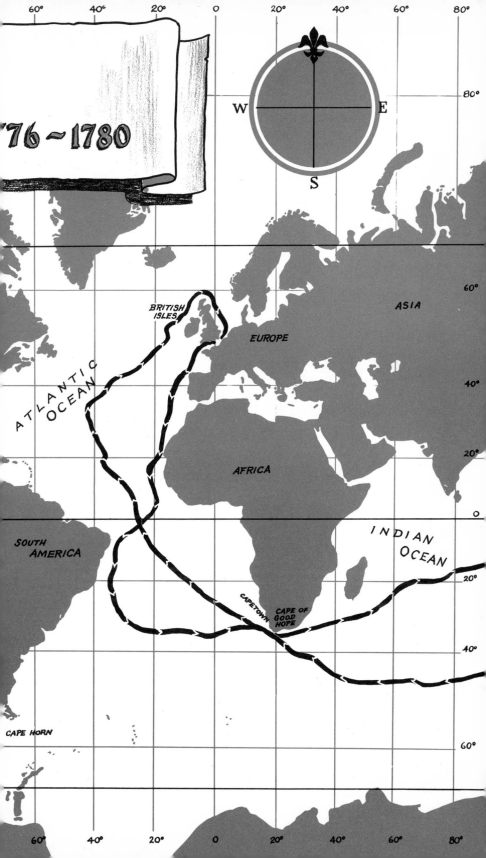

Third Voyage: 1776–1780
Is There a Northwest Passage?

There was great excitement in England when the *Resolution* sailed into port. For a whole year, ever since Captain Furneaux had returned, there were only wild guesses about its fate. Now Cook himself was back to tell his story. Honors were heaped on him as a national hero. He was promoted to the rank of captain. The famed Royal Society elected him a Fellow and his report on the prevention of scurvy at sea won the Society's Gold Medal as the best paper of the year. Cook's record was unheard of. He took more pride in conquering scurvy than he did in all of his geographical discoveries.

These honors went along with his appointment to a lifetime job—captain of Greenwich Hospital, an institution for retired naval men. Cook was uncertain about accepting this soft berth, which amounted to being pensioned off for life. He wrote to his old friend, Mr. Walker of Whitby, on whose collier he had first gone to sea as an apprentice: "A few months ago, the whole Southern Hemisphere was hardly enough for me." With an "active mind like mine," he asked, "how can I stand such narrow limits?" Cook concluded: "I must confess it is a fine retreat, and a pretty income, but whether I can bring myself to like ease and retirement time will show."

Time did not take long to show. After six months at home Cook's fate was sealed at a dinner party given by Lord Sandwich on February 9, 1776. The Admiralty was planning a new voyage but dared not ask Cook to lead it just after his six years at sea. At the dinner the conversation turned to the question that was disturbing the Admiralty. "Is there a Northwest Passage above Canada through which ships could pass from the Atlantic to the Pacific?"

During the age of Queen Elizabeth many explorers had searched for such a passage. But more was known now. The Dane, Vitus Bering, sailing for Peter the Great of Russia, had discovered that Asia and America were separated by a strait and that there was an Arctic Ocean above these two great continents. If an eastern entrance hadn't been discovered, maybe a western one could be.

The problem was becoming serious. The Spanish controlled the Isthmus of Panama and transshipment across it was difficult and uncertain. The trip around Cape Horn was perilous. Sailing around Africa was long and costly. The American colonies were in turmoil. The question of a shorter route to the Pacific was so critical that Parliament had voted a prize of £20,000 to the first man to discover it.

Cook's former lieutenant, Richard Pickersgill, was sailing in search of an eastern entrance. How valuable it would be if at the same time a ship should search for an entrance from the American Northwest! All that was needed was the right commander. Lord Sandwich asked for Cook's advice. Cook gave it. If their lordships were willing, he would go himself.

Cook presented himself at the Admiralty offices the next day to make a formal offer of his services. Before he left he had his commission drawn up, signed, and sealed. Back at home he wrote jubilantly to Mr. Walker: "I have quitted an easy retirement for an active, perhaps dangerous voyage— I embark on as fair a prospect as I can wish."

Cook had been working on the final draft of the *Journal* of his second voyage. There was still much editing and polishing to do. Little had he known when he started on these voyages that he was expected to be a writer, too! But he was now mastering that craft, just as he had those of navigation and surveying. At the same time he had been enjoying the companionship of his wife, Elizabeth, and their three boys, James, Nathaniel, and Hugh. The last of these he had never seen, as he was born the day before Cook sailed for the

Antarctic. Now all was suddenly changed. Cook had to plunge into the endless tasks of preparation.

Another Whitby collier was purchased to accompany the *Resolution*. Charles Clerke, who had been on Cook's two previous voyages, was put in command of the second ship, the *Discovery*. Cook's first lieutenant was John Gore, whom Cook himself had promoted on the *Endeavour*. His master was William Bligh, a strict, hard-bitten man who was later to become famous for the "mutiny on the *Bounty*." This time Cook was to double as commander and astronomer, while the surgeon, William Anderson, was to serve as both physician and naturalist. An official artist was sent along to record the most important scenes they might witness.

The two ships carried a complement of 192 officers and men, about whom there was something special that no one yet knew. Many of them had writing ambitions. There was a great popular demand for stories of such voyages as Cook's. The *Journal* of his first voyage had sold out the day it was published. The Forsters had already brought out, contrary to their agreement with the Admiralty, the story of the second voyage in two large volumes. They managed to get it printed before Cook's official Journal, which did not appear till after he was at sea again. This third voyage promised to be a big story. Some fifty journals of it were kept—one by every fourth man on board. Five of these, besides the official one, were published after the ships returned.

Two journals by an American and a German later

became widely known. One was by John Ledyard, the first American ever to see the Pacific Northwest. Ledyard had been at Dartmouth College for a short time studying for the ministry. Dissatisfied, he quit college and sailed to Europe as an ordinary seaman. In London he heard of Cook's planned voyage and determined to go on it. When he found there were no vacancies for seamen he enlisted in the marines and won Cook's acceptance.

The second journal was published by a German worker who, having drifted to London in search of a job, saw the possibility of high adventure and signed on the *Discovery*. This uneducated ordinary seaman, Henry Zimmerman, gave the world the best picture of Captain Cook as a man and a commander it has ever had.

Besides the search for a Northwest Passage, Cook's instructions required him to engage in many scientific tasks. He was to record the position of every place he saw and chart it. He was to examine the nature of the soil of every land he touched and to describe its produce, together with the animals and fowl that inhabited it. He was to look for "metals, minerals, or valuable stones" and to collect the seeds of all possible "trees, shrubs, plants, fruits, and grains." In addition to all this, he was to observe the people he met, "their genius, temper, disposition, and number" and "to endeavor by all proper means to cultivate a friendship with them . . . showing them every kind of civility and regard."

Those responsible were plainly determined that this voyage should advance Britain's knowledge of the world and prepare the ground for later British settlements. England was already at war with her American colonies and before Cook could sail from Plymouth they declared themselves independent. The Lords of the Admiralty were farseeing men.

The best-known American in Europe, Benjamin Franklin, was farseeing, too. When he issued instructions to the privateers he was hiring to prey on British shipping, he made one important exception. England had a ship at sea, he informed them, "to make discoveries of new countries in unknown seas, under the conduct of that most celebrated navigator and discoverer, Captain Cook." Inasmuch as such a voyage was "to the benefit of mankind in general," if any warships flying American colors should meet Cook's ship they were not to consider her an enemy but to assist her in any way possible, and to treat Cook and his people with kindness, "affording them, as common friends to mankind, all the assistance in your power which they may happen to stand in need of."

This was an extraordinary document. Cook's ship was a warship, if not a powerful one, and the American colonists were fighting for their lives against terrible odds. But Benjamin Franklin was wise in believing that both his country and mankind in general would be served by Cook's third voyage. He could not have known that this voyage was to help inspire the Lewis and Clark expedition and the development of the

Benjamin Franklin
issuing instructions

great Northwest and its fur trade, both through the influence, in part, of John Ledyard. Neither could Franklin possibly have envisioned the final American statehood of Alaska and Hawaii.

At last the expedition of the two little armed coal ships was ready to sail from Plymouth Harbor. The converted colliers looked strangely out of place amidst

the great men-of-war preparing to put down the rebel-
lion in America. Cook himself was moved by what he
called this "singular and affecting circumstance" that
while he was bound on an expedition for the benefit of
humanity, other ships of the same Navy were preparing to fight the American colonies. This "affecting cir-

cumstance" was strongly accented on July 6, 1776, when three great British warships, escorting a fleet of sixty-two transports loaded with mercenary Hessian troops, stopped at Plymouth on their way to America. Six days later Cook sailed out of the harbor on his peaceful mission of discovery.

After a stop at Cape Town, the last civilized port of call Cook expected to see for three years, the two ships sailed around the Cape of Good Hope and crossed the South Pacific to Queen Charlotte's Sound. At their familiar anchorage the usual friendly exchange of nose-rubbing with their old Maori acquaintances was restrained. All were only too conscious of the massacre of Furneaux's boat crew. The ringleader was pointed out to Cook and even confessed that he had killed the commanding officer. Many of the English and even some of the Maoris thought Cook ought to avenge the death of his countrymen. As Cook pieced together the story, it was another of those ever-recurring cases of theft. Maoris stole some clothes of the boat's crew. The English fired at them till their ammunition was gone. Then, in revenge for the killing of their people, the Maoris attacked. Cook had no heart for punishing these people, for savages, he frequently said, "never commit murder without provocation."

Cook sailed from New Zealand the end of February 1777, hoping to get to the Arctic that summer. He needed the months of June, July, and August for explorations in the far north. But the winds and weather were against him. It was nearly nine thousand miles from New Zealand to Bering Strait and he couldn't sail that distance in time. There was nothing to do but try to make more discoveries in the Pacific. Cook did. He discovered a group of islands completely unknown to Europeans that lay some six hundred miles west of Tahiti. These are now known as the Cook Islands. Then they spent nine months at the Friendly Islands, which they had found so delightful on the previous voyage.

The months were spent in preparation for the voyage ahead, combined with feasting and dancing. The sailors and the friendly inhabitants outdid each other in hospitality. One enthusiastic sailor wrote, "A more civilized people does not exist under the sun." Here was the eighteenth-century European idea of the "noble savage" completely fulfilled.

While others off duty made merry, Cook used his time to observe and describe the life, habits, and religion of these people. Why, he would ask himself, do different people in these different lands have the customs,

beliefs, traditions they do? What makes some hostile, others friendly? Why are some cannibals, while others are horrified at cannibalism? Why are some peoples so open and friendly, others suspicious and resentful? And what, he asked, is the relationship between their dealings among themselves and the way they act toward their visitors?

Cook was as careful and as scientific in his study of the people he met—a study now called ethnology or cultural anthropology—as he was in his navigation. And, as seaman Zimmerman reported, he loved these peoples of the Pacific "and was never happier than in association with them."

The Hawaiian Islands Discovered

Then they sailed off from all these lovely and familiar islands into the unknown waters of the northern Pacific. At daybreak on January 18, 1778, there was a surprised cry of "Land Ho!" from the masthead.

New uncharted islands were sighted. They turned out to be the Hawaiian Islands, never before seen by Europeans. Canoes surrounded them and the visitors were delighted to see that these were the same kind of people as at Tahiti and the Friendly Islands. Those not in canoes swam all about the ships. They were as much at home in the water as on land.

After a party was sent ashore to get water, Cook, accompanied by Dr. Anderson, the surgeon-naturalist, and Mr. Webber, the painter, went ashore. When the tall, handsome Cook, in his blue and white gold-braided uniform, leaped from the boat, the hundreds of Hawaiians on shore fell flat to the ground and prostrated themselves before him. As they walked inland with a Hawaiian as a guide, those behind rose to their feet and turned around to see and follow Cook. When he turned to look back all fell flat on their faces again. What did they take this strange white visitor to be? Was he another great chief, or a god who had come from the sun or moon?

This was a rare new land. Cook was glad the

Spaniards had never discovered it, for it would make a marvelous stopping point for ships sailing between America and Asia. He found five islands and recorded the native names by which they are known today. Not till the following year did Cook see the largest of this island group. The natives called this one Hawaii. He named the whole group the *Sandwich Islands* after the First Lord of the Admiralty.

Cook was deeply impressed that the people were of the same "nation" as the Tahitians and spoke a similar language. He was the first person to observe that these same people, now called Polynesians, had spread by means of their marvelously made canoes over the vast area from New Zealand to Hawaii and from Easter Island to the Hebrides. That meant they occupied islands stretching through 3600 miles of ocean from north to south and about 5000 miles from east to west.

Into the Arctic

A month later, highly pleased with their discovery, the two ships sailed from this island group for the coast of America. They reached it at what is now Oregon and sailed north, searching for any possible passage to the east. They found new kinds of Indians and marveled at their great carved totem poles. They cruised north, mapping the coast all the while, until in Alaska they came to a great river or inlet that looked like a possible opening to the east. They sailed up this water

Indian totem poles

a hundred miles or so, only to find the mountains slowly closing in on them. Cook landed not far from where Anchorage now stands and claimed the region for Britain. Then they sailed through the Aleutian Island chain and through the strait Bering discovered.

Here, beyond the Arctic Circle, was plainly the last chance for a passage to the east and probably to

At Kamchatka

the west as well. Was there an open sea passage, or would they be stopped by a wall of ice? As in the Antarctic, Cook found nearly continuous fog and snow in midsummer, as he tacked back and forth between the American and Siberian coasts, trying to get through the impenetrable ice pack. Way up in latitude 70° 44′ North, the fog lifted only to reveal a wall of ice ten or

106

twelve feet high. Finally, on August 29, Cook was forced to give up the search. He would winter in the convenient Sandwich or Hawaiian Islands and try again the following summer. Winter was now closing in and there was too much danger of becoming frozen in a solid sea of ice.

They had not discovered a Northwest Passage but they had confirmed Bering's discoveries and had mapped 3500 miles of the unknown western coast of North America above the area the Spanish had explored.

Down they sailed along the Russian coast of Kamchatka, sometimes enjoying the hospitality of the Russian fur traders. But the *Resolution* was leaking badly from rotten planking, her masts were rotting, too, and her sails were in a sorry plight. Cook had made one of his few serious blunders in accepting her for this voyage. The previous one in the Antarctic had been all she could take. To make matters worse, Surgeon Anderson had died of tuberculosis in the Arctic and Captain Clerke was so ill with it that often he could barely walk.

Cook: An Hawaiian God?

At last they reached the Hawaiian Islands. This time they coasted along the largest one, Hawaii itself. After days of search for a good harbor they anchored

107

in Kealakekua Bay on its west coast. In the distance was the great snow-covered volcano of Mauna Loa. It was toward noon on January 17, 1779 that Cook ordered the sails unbent and the yards struck.

The scene that greeted them was unbelievable. The Hawaiians swarmed over the ships. Hundreds upon hundreds swam about them. Many hundreds more of the friendly people surrounded them in canoes. Thousands packed the shore. A priest named Koah invited Cook ashore and took him to a large holy place. "The other gentlemen, with Pareea, a young chief, and four or five more of the natives followed."

These were the last words Cook wrote. His own journal broke off abruptly here. The rest of the official story was written by Lieutenant King, who completed the journal of the third voyage.

Cook's few last written words give but a pale glimpse of what really happened. When Cook's ships appeared in Kealakekua Bay word spread that Rono, the god of peace and prosperity, had returned. Ages before he had sailed from these shores with the promise that he would come back. He would return, Rono had said, in a large ship with a small forest of trees in her, and sail into the Bay of Rainbows (Kealakekua). Now he was here. Cook was believed to be the long-awaited Rono.

When Cook stepped ashore that day, the chiefs holding long poles cried out, "The great Rono is coming." Ten thousand people shouted, covered their faces with their hands, and prostrated themselves on the

ground. On the walk up to the village, those on the ground in front of Cook were constantly in danger of being trampled on by those behind who had already risen to follow the procession. As the walk continued they hit upon the idea of following Cook on all fours. In this way Cook was conducted to the *morai* or holy

place. Here an elaborate religious ceremony was held in an enclosure surrounded by a wooden rail to which were fixed skulls of those who had been sacrificed to the gods. In this strange situation there was nothing for Cook to do but to participate in all solemnity.

Before many days an idol was erected to Cook. They called it "Orono no te tuti," meaning Cook the God Rono, "tuti" being their word for Cook. Later on when the astronomer of the *Discovery,* Cook, and Lieutenant King set up their telescopes and quadrants on shore and occupied themselves with watching the sun, moon and planets, the Hawaiians were even more convinced that their visitors must have come from these heavenly bodies. That they could kill birds with fire without themselves being hurt by it was also a powerful argument for their being gods.

The chiefs and priests saw to it that the great white God-chief and his followers were provided with all the food they needed. The people obliged. But those who had shouted on the first day, "Ehri no te tuti Mai tai" or, "The Beloved Chief Cook is good," were not prepared for so long a visit. The strangers stayed on. The 190 men on the two ships needed a stupendous quantity of food. They were not only underfed to begin with

but were storing food away for the coming year. A thirteen-month ration of pork for both ships was salted away. Entertaining the white gods was becoming costly.

Food may have been plentiful on the island, but there was a limit to it. The Hawaiians started to stroke the sides and pat the bellies of the sailors, telling them in sign language that they were now fat and it was time for them to go.

One of the biggest chiefs of the islands, King Terreeoboo, who had welcomed them warmly when they first came, now began to ask when they would leave. Cook was unsure what this meant. Did King Terreeoboo want them to leave, or did he merely want to know when they would be going so that he could give them farewell presents?

On February 2, 1779, the carpenters finished the necessary repairs. Cook told the king he would leave the day after tomorrow. Immediately a proclamation was issued throughout the villages. The people were to bring in hogs and vegetables for the king to present to Cook on his departure.

On February 4 the two ships sailed out of Kealakekua Bay, after the warmest farewells on both sides. But three days out at sea a gale hit them and the foremast of the *Resolution* split. There was no other way. They had to return to Kealakekua Bay to repair the mast.

The Death of Captain Cook

Back at the bay, things did not look right. Their reception was suspiciously quiet. No Hawaiians swarmed over the ships. There was hardly a canoe on the bay. The people seemed to have been ordered to stay away.

The next day the taboo was lifted and again the Hawaiians were friendly. For a few days things went along quietly. Then, on February 13th, a group of natives on board the *Discovery* stole the armorer's tongs from the ship's forge and set off with them in a canoe belonging to a young chief, Pareea. The Englishmen chased them to the shore, recovered the tongs and tried to seize the canoe. Pareea arrived. Insisting he had nothing to do with the theft, he resisted. In the ensuing scuffle Pareea was knocked down by a blow on the head with an oar. Immediately the Hawaiians who had collected began to attack with stones. The English had to retreat.

At daybreak the following morning, seaman Zimmerman, while making his rounds as deck watch on the *Discovery*, found that their best boat was missing from the buoy where it was moored. Word of the missing boat was immediately sent over to Captain Cook on the *Resolution*. Cook's belief in the necessity of the cutter for their coming voyage into the Arctic made him determine to recover it immediately. In a violent temper, he decided to use a method he had employed a number of times before to recover important stolen articles. He would go on shore and persuade King Terreeoboo to come on board. Then he would hold him on the ship as a hostage till the boat was returned. He ordered the boats manned and their men armed with muskets and side arms. One was to take him ashore with nine marines. Others were to guard the harbor and prevent any canoes from leaving or coming in. The situation was clearly dangerous, as the damaged foremast of the *Resolution* was being repaired on shore, the sailmakers were repairing the sails there, and the astronomical instruments had been set up again.

Cook landed shortly after seven o'clock in the morning. Dressed in full uniform and carrying a musket, he walked into the village. Behind him were nine marines carrying guns. Cook was showing the islanders that he meant business.

He found the house where aged King Terreeoboo had passed the night. Cook invited him to spend the day on the *Resolution*. The king readily agreed, and got up from his mat on the floor to follow Cook. His two sons and several others of the king's retinue followed. Everything went well until they neared the beach. There an elderly woman, one of Terreeoboo's favorite

114

wives, dropped to her knees before him and begged him with tears in her eyes not to go on board. At the same time two chiefs took the king's arms. They insisted he go no farther, and forced him to sit down. By this time a huge crowd of islanders had gathered around Cook and their king.

Cook continued to entreat the king to follow. Several times the king started to get up. But each time the chiefs closed in and insisted he not go. Finally Cook, realizing that the fear and alarm were too great, turned to Lieutenant Phillips and said, "We can't do it. It is impossible to compel the king to go with us without killing too many of these people."

Cook left the seated king and walked slowly toward the shore. Just then a man came running from the other side of the bay, almost breathless. Panting, he exclaimed: "It is war! The foreigners have commenced hostilities, have fired on a canoe from one of the boats and killed a chief." Quick as wildfire the message ran through the crowd.

The people stirred angrily. The women and children slipped away. The men put on war mats and armed themselves with spears and stones. Cook, threatened with an iron spike, shot and killed a Hawaiian. A real attack with stones began, and both the marines with Cook and those in the boats fired their muskets. The islanders were expected to melt back. Instead they stood firm, and before the marines had time to reload they rushed forward with shouts and yells. Four of the marines were killed and three more seriously wounded.

At this moment Cook was standing at the water's edge with his back to the crowd, signaling to his boats to draw in. His one aim seems to have been to withdraw and avoid more bloodshed. Just then a chief stole up behind him and stabbed him in the back. Cook fell with his face in the water. A great shout went up from the crowd and his body was immediately dragged on shore and surrounded by the islanders. The rest of the

marines threw themselves into the water and escaped under cover of gunfire from the boats. But the great Commander was dead!

Many of the crew and officers wanted vengeance. There were proposals to shell and burn the village. But Cook's own spirit prevailed among the officers. They sought only to get the mast, sails, and astronomical instruments back on board and to recover Cook's body.

Lieutenant King succeeded in arranging a truce to get their materials back on board. At the same time he patiently sought to get the Hawaiians to return Cook's body. But in the intervening time they had paid funeral honors to Cook in their own way. His body had been dismembered and distributed among a number of chiefs and priests to be used in religious ceremonies. Within twenty-four hours of his death different parts of Cook's body were traveling in different directions over the island. He was still the God Rono and his death was mourned by the Hawaiians, even though they were bitter at the English for the death of six of their chiefs. Many asked: "When will Rono come again?" Some wanted him to come back. Others feared the vengeance he might take on them. King Terreeoboo wanted peace, and his own son returned some of Cook's bones wrapped in fine new cloth and covered with a beautiful cloak of black and white feathers. At last, having got all the remains of Cook they were likely to get, there was nothing more to do than to perform the funeral services.

One week after the tragedy, on Sunday, February

119

21, the ships lowered their colors to half mast. At the request of the English, Hawaiian priests put the bay under a taboo so it was completely deserted. Officers and men lined up on deck. Just as the sun set Captain Clerke read the funeral service and the coffin was lowered over the side with the accompaniment of a ten-gun salute. They all cried like children. The life and heart had gone out of the expedition.

The day after Cook's funeral, the two ships sailed out of the Hawaiian bay. Captain Clerke was now in command. Lieutenant Gore took Clerke's place as commander of the *Discovery*. The officers had little heart for it, but they decided to carry out Cook's plan for another search that summer for the Northwest Passage.

It was more or less a token expedition. As seaman Zimmerman wrote, "The spirit of adventure, the energy and steady courage were lost."

Back at Kamchatka Peninsula they were again entertained hospitably by the Russians, who promised

to send overland a letter Captain Clerke had written to the Lords of the Admiralty. This letter was carried nearly ten thousand miles across Asia and Europe and

reached London six months before the ships arrived. The newspapers immediately informed London and the world of Cook's tragic death.

In spite of the bad state of the *Resolution* and the fact that Captain Clerke was hopelessly ill, they sailed once again into the Arctic Ocean. They tried to pay tribute to Cook by sailing farther than he had done the previous summer. But this proved impossible. The pack ice threatened to close them in. The *Discovery* was actually frozen in the ice for a time and badly damaged. They were all heartily sick of this dangerous voyage and delighted when the ships were finally ordered home. They had been out three whole years and knew that it would take another whole year to reach England. Clerke died before they returned to Kamchatka and Gore took command. He got the ships safely home to Deptford on the Thames October 6, 1780. It was just four years and three months since they had proudly sailed out of Plymouth.

Mourning and Monuments

James Cook's death at the age of fifty was deeply mourned. King George cried when he heard the news. Sir Hugh Palliser, under whom Cook had sailed for such a long time as a noncommissioned officer, did a most extraordinary thing. He erected a monument to Cook on his country estate. It was a block of marble surmounted by a globe of the world. On the block he had inscribed: "To the memory of Captain James Cook, the Ablest and Most Renowned Navigator This or Any Country hath produced." Today a statue of Cook stands in front of the Admiralty in London. Another one stands on the shore of Kealakekua Bay to mark the spot where Cook fell.

Many tributes to Cook were paid by men who had sailed with him, from the aristocratic Joseph Banks, who became president of the Royal Society, to the ordinary German seaman, Henry Zimmerman. All agree on Cook's basic character. He kept himself aloof and spoke little. He never had a really intimate friend, even though he was respected and admired by his superiors, his subordinates, and the countless Pacific islanders whose acquaintance he made and whose company he always seemed to prefer to that of his countrymen. He himself, perhaps, would have liked best the tribute of the sister of one of his lieutenants. The novelist, Fanny Burney, one of the "great ladies" of the day, wrote of Cook in her diary: "He was the most moderate, humane and gentle navigator who ever went out upon discoveries." Cook had great physical courage and astonishing self-discipline. He asked much of his officers and men, but he always asked them less than he demanded of himself. His life was his work and his work was to explore.

The Royal Society issued a gold medal in honor of its distinguished member. Cook's profile was on one side and the figure of Britannia holding a globe on the other. Copies were presented to King George and Queen Charlotte, to Lord Sandwich, to Mrs. Cook, to the King of France, the Empress of Russia, and to one of the leaders of the American Revolution, Dr. Benjamin Franklin.

Mrs. Cook lived to the age of ninety-four. During all their seventeen years of marriage, she and her husband had been together a total of about four years. She lived a lonely and tragic life. Their daughter, Elizabeth, had died at the age of four, while Cook was on his first voyage. Within a year of the news of her husband's death her son Nathaniel, age sixteen, was drowned in a Navy vessel. Nine years later her youngest son, Hugh, died of diptheria soon after entering Cambridge University. Her oldest son, James, who was an officer in the Navy and commander of a warship, drowned at the age of thirty-two when his ship went down in a storm.

The life of Captain Cook's family was tragic, but his own life was not. His great passion was navigation in uncharted waters, and this he accomplished nobly. As his lieutenant, James King, wrote, Cook's death "cannot be reckoned premature, since he lived to finish the great work for which he seems to have been designed."

His greatest monument, it has been said, is the map of the Pacific. But equally great was his conquest of scurvy and his introduction of a new age of scientific exploration. He was the last of the great classic explorers, and the first of the moderns. With Cook a new line of world explorer, mapmaker, and scientist began. His successors were Bellingshausen, Vancouver, Humboldt, Amundsen, Scott, and Peary.

Coat of arms bestowed on Cook's family

Index